The Five Senses

Tasting

Rebecca Rissman

www.heinemannlibrary.co.uk
Visit our website to find out more information about Heinemann Library books.

To order:

☎ Phone +44 (0) 1865 888066

🖹 Fax +44 (0) 1865 314091

🖥 Visit www.heinemannlibrary.co.uk

Edited by Rebecca Rissman and Catherine Veitch
Designed by Ryan Frieson and Kimberly R. Miracle
Original illustrations © Capstone Global Library
Illustrated by Tony Wilson (pp. 11, 22)
Picture research by Tracy Cummins
Originated by Capstone Global Library
Printed in China by South China Printing Company Ltd

ISBN 978 0 431194 82 0
14 13 12 11 10
10 9 8 7 6 5 4 3 2 1

British Library Cataloguing in Publication Data
Rissman, Rebecca
Tasting. -- (The Five Senses)
612.8'7--dc22
A full catalogue record for this book is available from the British Library.

Acknowledgments
The author and publishers are grateful to the following for permission to reproduce copyright material: Alamy p. 21 (© Andrew Fox); Corbis pp. 7 (© Don Mason), 10 (© Heide Benser); Getty Images pp. 6 (ABSODELS), 12 (Eric Millette), 13 (Robert Warren), 14 (Bambu Productions), 16 (Robert Daly), 17 (AE Pictures Inc.); istockphoto p. 8 (alvarez); Photolibrary p. 18 (Digital Vision); Shutterstock pp. 4 (© Sergey Pristyazhnyuk), 5 (© topal), 9 (© Victor Newman), 15 (© Monkey Business Images), 19 (© goldenangel), 20 (© nateperro), 23 A (© goldenangel), 23 B (© topal), 23 C (© Victor Newman), 23D (© nateperro).

Cover photograph of a boy eating a watermelon reproduced with permission of Getty Images (ColorBlind Images). Back cover photograph of a girl eating meat reproduced with permission of Shutterstock (© nateperro).

The publishers would like to thank Nancy Harris, Yael Biederman, and Matt Siegel for their assistance in the preparation of this book.

Every effort has been made to contact copyright holders of any material reproduced in this book. Any omissions will be rectified in subsequent printings if notice is given to the publisher.

Contents

Senses

We all have five senses.

We use our senses every day.

Tasting and smelling are senses.

Seeing, hearing, and touching are also senses.

How do you taste?

mouth

You use your mouth to taste.

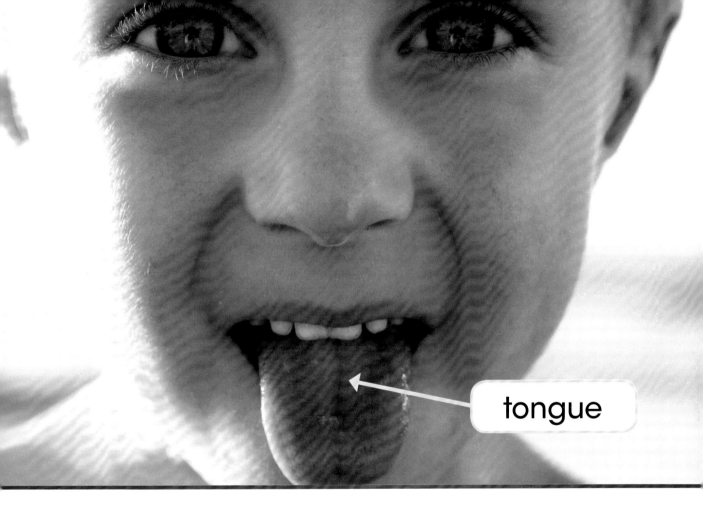

tongue

Your tongue helps you to taste.

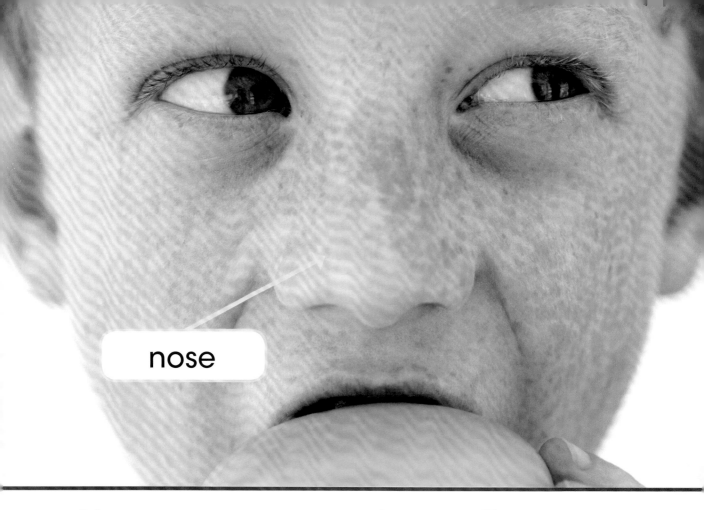

nose

You use your nose to smell.

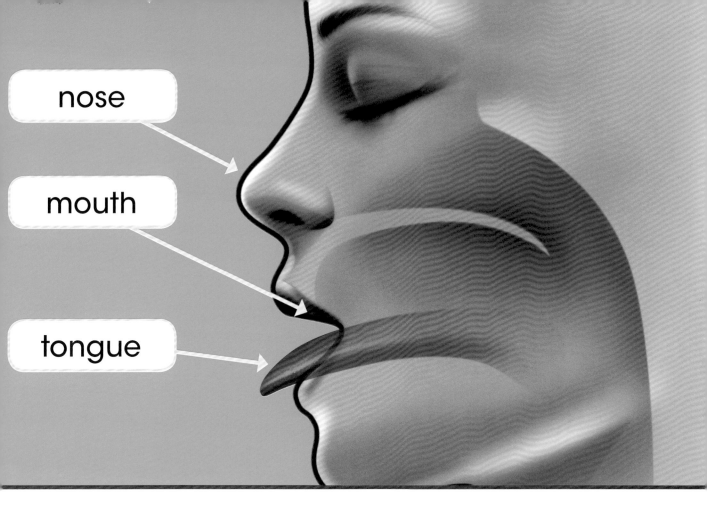

nose

mouth

tongue

Together your mouth, tongue, and nose help you to taste.

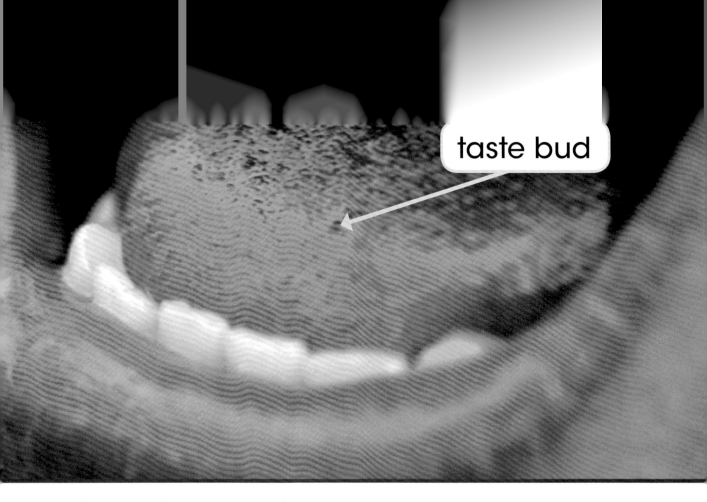

taste bud

Your tongue is covered in taste buds.

Taste buds help you taste
different things.

What do you taste?

You can taste food and drinks.

You can taste five main flavours.

You can taste sour flavours. Lemons taste sour.

You can taste bitter flavours. Olives taste bitter.

You can taste salty flavours. Popcorn
can taste salty.

You can taste sweet flavours. Some fruits taste sweet.

You can taste umami flavours.
Umami is a meaty flavour.

You can taste many flavours at the same time.

Naming the parts you use to taste

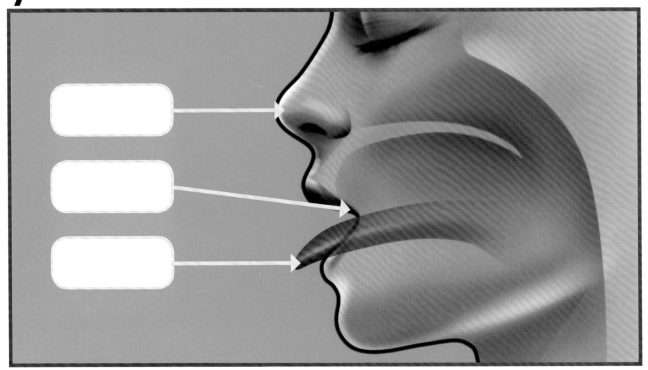

Point to where these labels should go.

nose   mouth   tongue

Answer on page 11.

Picture glossary

flavour the taste and smell that something has

sense something that helps you smell, see, touch, taste, or hear things around you

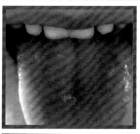

taste buds tiny parts on your tongue that help you to taste different things

umami meaty flavour

Index

Note to parents and teachers

Before reading

Explain to children that people use five senses to understand the world: seeing, hearing, tasting, touching, and smelling. Tell children that there are different body parts associated with each sense. Then ask children which body parts they think they use to taste. Tell children that they use their mouth, tongue, and nose to taste flavours.

After reading

• Show children the diagram of the sensory system on page 22. Ask them to point to where the labels "mouth", "tongue", and "nose" should go.

• Write the five flavours on the board: salty, sweet, sour, bitter, and umami. Then ask children to list foods that fall under each flavour category.

• Ask each child to write their favourite food on a small piece of paper. Then tape these pieces of paper on the board to form a bar chart of the classes favourite foods.